LITTLE WOMEN
the musical

T0066293

CONTENTS

Piano/vocal arrangements by Jason Howland and David Pearl

Cherry Lane Music Company
Director of Publications/Project Editor: Mark Phillips

ISBN 978-1-60378-261-6

Visit our website at www.cherrylaneprint.com

Our Finest Dreams

Lyrics by
Mindi Dickstein

Music by
Jason Howland

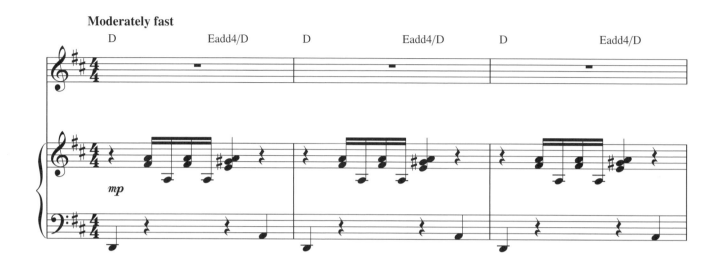

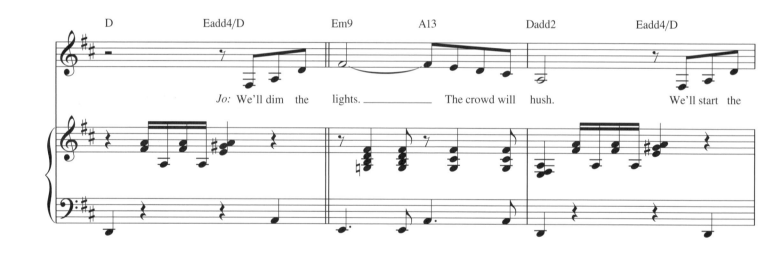

Jo: We'll dim the lights. _____ The crowd will hush. We'll start the
o - ver - ture and Beth will sure - ly blush. And when Cla - ris - sa starts to

cries. _____ I know you're tired. _____ I know it's

hard. But we will tri - umph when Rod - ri - go yells *"en - garde." ("Tou - ché!")* Our suc -

cess is guar - an - teed! Christ - mas will be thrill - ing.

Christ - mas will be go - ry. Christ - mas will ex - ceed our fin - est dreams.

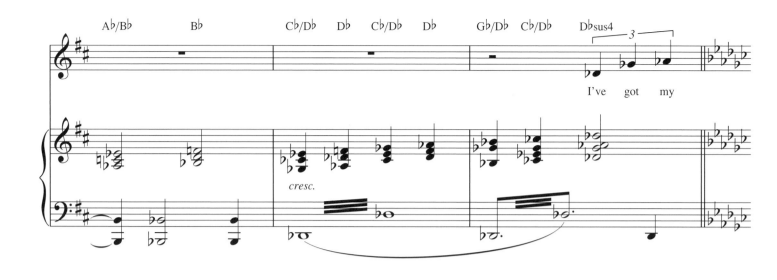

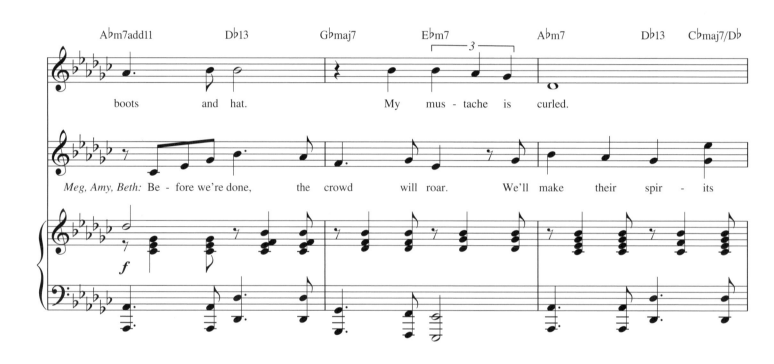

Here Alone

Words by
Mindi Dickstein

Music by
Jason Howland

Take a Chance on Me

Lyrics by
Mindi Dickstein

Music by
Jason Howland

19

G♭add2 We could live _____ a mil - lion dreams, _____ but

Five Forever

Words by
Mindi Dickstein

Music by
Jason Howland

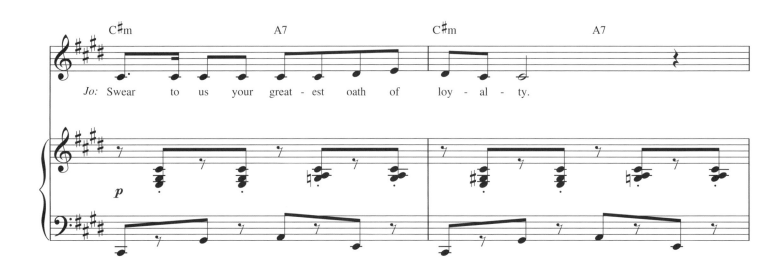

28

day,

Meg, Beth, Amy, Jo: (It's won - der - ful.

one I'll nev - er for - get,

Nev - er for -

I am hon - ored to say

get. Ah.)

I am yours.

Astonishing

Words by
Mindi Dickstein

Music by
Jason Howland

Some Things Are Meant to Be

Lyrics by
Mindi Dickstein

Music by
Jason Howland

meant to be: The tide turn-ing end-less-ly. The way it takes hold of me. No

mat-ter what I do. But some things will nev-er die: the prom-ise of

who you are, your mem-'ries when I am far from you.

Slower, freely

All my life I've lived for __ lov-ing you. Let me go now.

Days of Plenty

Lyrics by
Mindi Dickstein

Music by
Jason Howland

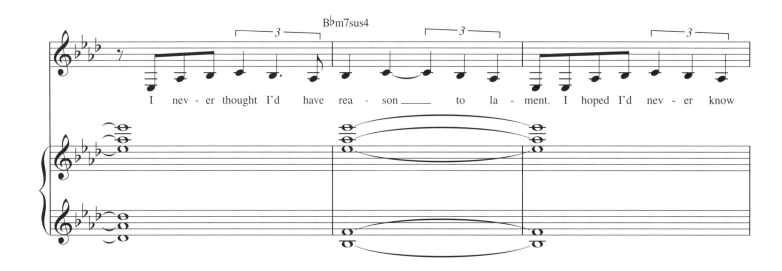

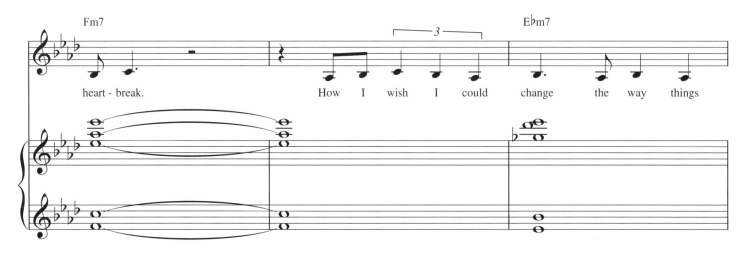

49

Small Umbrella in the Rain

Words by
Mindi Dickstein

Music by
Jason Howland

pas-sion to share, _____ I think we have more than e-nough, e-nough to make a mar-riage, if we

dare. _____ *(Spoken:)* *Jo: You are proposing?* *P.B.: No. Yes! Yes!* *I do not mean today, or tomorrow,*

or even next month, a year. Maybe two years, even. I'm a patient man. *Jo:* I won't be sweet, won't be de-

mure. *J.B.: This* I pre-fer, this I a-dore. *Jo:* I'll speak my mind, you can be

More Great Piano/Vocal Books
FROM CHERRY LANE

For a complete listing of Cherry Lane titles available,
including contents listings, please visit our web site at
www.cherrylane.com

02501590	Sara Bareilles – Kaleidoscope Heart	$17.99
02501136	Sara Bareilles – Little Voice	$16.95
02501505	The Black Eyed Peas – The E.N.D.	$19.99
02502171	The Best of Boston	$17.95
02501614	Zac Brown Band – The Foundation	$19.99
02501618	Zac Brown Band – You Get What You Give	$19.99
02501123	Buffy the Vampire Slayer – Once More with Feeling	$18.95
02500665	Sammy Cahn Songbook	$24.95
02501688	Colbie Caillat – All of You	$17.99
02501454	Colbie Caillat – Breakthrough	$17.99
02501127	Colbie Caillat – Coco	$16.95
02500144	Mary Chapin Carpenter – Party Doll & Other Favorites	$16.95
02500838	Best of Joe Cocker	$16.95
02502165	John Denver Anthology – Revised	$22.95
02500002	John Denver Christmas	$14.95
02502166	John Denver's Greatest Hits	$17.95
02502151	John Denver – A Legacy in Song (Softcover)	$24.95
02500566	Poems, Prayers and Promises: The Art and Soul of John Denver	$19.95
02500326	John Denver – The Wildlife Concert	$17.95
02500501	John Denver and the Muppets: A Christmas Together	$9.95
02501186	The Dresden Dolls – The Virginia Companion	$39.95
02509922	The Songs of Bob Dylan	$29.95
02500497	Linda Eder – Gold	$14.95
02500396	Linda Eder – Christmas Stays the Same	$17.95
02502209	Linda Eder – It's Time	$17.95
02501542	Foreigner – The Collection	$19.99
02500535	Erroll Garner Anthology	$19.95
02500318	Gladiator	$12.95
02502126	Best of Guns N' Roses	$17.95
02502072	Guns N' Roses – Selections from Use Your Illusion I and II	$17.95
02500014	Sir Roland Hanna Collection	$19.95
02501447	Eric Hutchinson – Sounds Like This	$17.99
02500856	Jack Johnson – Anthology	$19.95
02501140	Jack Johnson – Sleep Through the Static	$16.95

02501564	Jack Johnson – To the Sea	$19.99
02501546	Jack's Mannequin – *The Glass Passenger* and *The Dear Jack EP*	$19.99
02500834	The Best of Rickie Lee Jones	$16.95
02500381	Lenny Kravitz – Greatest Hits	$14.95
02501318	John Legend – Evolver	$19.99
02500822	John Legend – Get Lifted	$16.99
02503701	Man of La Mancha	$11.95
02501047	Dave Matthews Band – Anthology	$24.95
02500693	Dave Matthews – Some Devil	$16.95
02502192	Dave Matthews Band – Under the Table and Dreaming	$17.95
02501514	John Mayer Anthology – Volume 1	$22.99
02501504	John Mayer – Battle Studies	$19.99
02500987	John Mayer – Continuum	$16.95
02500681	John Mayer – Heavier Things	$16.95
02500563	John Mayer – Room for Squares	$16.95
02500081	Natalie Merchant – Ophelia	$14.95
02500863	Jason Mraz – Mr. A-Z	$17.95
02501467	Jason Mraz – We Sing. We Dance. We Steal Things.	$19.99
02502895	Nine	$17.95
02501411	Nine – Film Selections	$19.99
02500425	Time and Love: The Art and Soul of Laura Nyro	$21.95
02502204	The Best of Metallica	$17.95
02501497	Ingrid Michaelson – Everybody	$17.99
02501496	Ingrid Michaelson – Girls and Boys	$19.99
02501768	Ingrid Michaelson – Human Again	$17.99
02501529	Monte Montgomery Collection	$24.99
02500857	Anna Nalick – Wreck of the Day	$16.95
02501336	Amanda Palmer – Who Killed Amanda Palmer?	$17.99
02501004	Best of Gram Parsons	$16.95
02500010	Tom Paxton – The Honor of Your Company	$17.95
02507962	Peter, Paul & Mary – Holiday Concert	$17.95
02500145	Pokemon 2.B.A. Master	$12.95
02500026	The Prince of Egypt	$16.95
02500660	Best of Bonnie Raitt	$17.95
02502189	The Bonnie Raitt Collection	$22.95
02502088	Bonnie Raitt – Luck of the Draw	$14.95
02507958	Bonnie Raitt – Nick of Time	$14.95
02502218	Kenny Rogers – The Gift	$16.95
02501577	She & Him – Volume One	$16.99

02501578	She & Him – Volume Two	$16.99
02500414	Shrek	$16.99
02500536	Spirit – Stallion of the Cimarron	$16.95
02500166	Steely Dan – Anthology	$17.95
02500622	Steely Dan – Everything Must Go	$14.95
02500284	Steely Dan – Two Against Nature	$14.95
02500344	Billy Strayhorn: An American Master	$17.95
02500515	Barbra Streisand – Christmas Memories	$16.95
02502164	Barbra Streisand – The Concert	$22.95
02500550	Essential Barbra Streisand	$24.95
02502228	Barbra Streisand – Higher Ground	$17.99
02501065	Barbra Streisand – Live in Concert 2006	$19.95
02501485	Barbra Streisand – Love Is the Answer	$19.99
02502178	The John Tesh Collection	$17.95
02503623	John Tesh – A Family Christmas	$15.95
02503630	John Tesh – Grand Passion	$16.95
02500307	John Tesh – Pure Movies 2	$16.95
02501068	The Evolution of Robin Thicke	$19.95
02500565	Thoroughly Modern Millie	$17.99
02501399	Best of Toto	$19.99
02502175	Tower of Power – Silver Anniversary	$17.95
02501403	Keith Urban – Defying Gravity	$17.99
02501008	Keith Urban – Love, Pain & The Whole Crazy Thing	$17.95
02501141	Keith Urban – Greatest Hits	$16.99
02502198	The "Weird Al" Yankovic Anthology	$17.95
02500334	Maury Yeston – December Songs	$17.95
02502225	The Maury Yeston Songbook	$19.95

See your local music dealer or contact:

EXCLUSIVELY DISTRIBUTED BY

7777 W. BLUEMOUND RD. P.O. BOX 13819 MILWAUKEE, WI 53213

Prices, contents and availability subject to change without notice.

0512